Surfing the Tsunami

by kelly giles

featuring cover art by Mark Moya

Limited first edition

First published February 2012

www.kgstoryteller.com

www.booksbyprescription.com

Copyright 2012 Kelly Giles

All rights reserved.

ISBN 978-0-578-08801-3

"What is to give light must endure burning."
- Victor Frankl, concentration camp survivor, psychotherapist, and author of "Man's Search for Meaning.

"The wound is the place where the Light enters you."
-Rumi

We must embrace pain and burn it as fuel for our journey. ~Kenji Miyazawa

Adversity is like a strong wind. It tears away from us all but the things that cannot be torn, so that we see ourselves as we really are. ~Arthur Golden, *Memoirs of a Geisha*

When it is dark enough, you can see the stars. ~Ralph Waldo Emerson

Smooth seas do not make skillful sailors. ~African Proverb

He who has a why to live can bear almost any how. ~Friedrich Nietzsche

Against criticism a man can neither protest nor defend himself; he must act in spite of it, and then it will gradually yield to him. ~Johann Wolfgang von Goethe, *Maxims and Reflections*

Perhaps all the dragons of our lives are princesses who are only waiting to see us once beautiful and brave. ~Rainer Maria Rilke

Embracing alienation 2

Acknowledging alienation
    Brutally broken
Criminally compassionate
    Deafness debilitates
Embraces emptiness
    Forgiven failure
Grasps grace
    Hides hopelessness
Imagines innocence
    Loses liberty
Misses mercy
    Numbs neediness
Openly oppressed
    Poverty paralyzes
Ruined reputation
    Stricken shepherd
Terrifyingly trusting
    Unimaginably undermined
Valiantly visionary
    Welcomes weakness
Hobbles homeward

Glimpsing glimmers

Familiarity fades

　　　Unimaginably uncertain

Ruined rescuer

　　　Fainting fighter

Weary walker

　　　Ragged runner

Lost liberty

　　　Blindness brutalizes

Glimpses glimmers

　　　Threats terrorize

Deafness demonizes

　　　Powerlessness paralyzes

Defiance dignifies

　　　Rebellious rescuer

Faces fears

　　　Transcends trauma

Grasps grace

Angelic anguish

Demands divide

    Desires inspire

Leaving liberates

    Teaches trust

Divine dependence

    Brutally betrayed

Bulletproof heart

    Abandonment's anguish

Fears fragility

    Angelically adopted

Suicidal survivor

    Illusions isolate

Creatively chaotic

    Control corrupts

Surrender saves

    Welcomes wonder

Compassionately wounded

Wounded trust

      Shattered self-sufficiency

Brutally betrayed

      Traumatically torn

Desperately driven

      Selflessly slaughtered

Neediness neglected

      Achingly abandoned

Frighteningly fragile

      Compassionately cradled

Façade fragments

Avoids abandonment

    Buries brokenness

Calmly chaotic

    Desperately driven

Escapes emptiness

    Fears fragility

Glimpses grace

    Hides heart

Inspiringly insecure

    Jams joyously

Loses liberty

    Masks misery

Numbs neediness

    Orphans openness

Painfully perceptive

    Quietly questions

Routinely rebels

    Silently screams

Tentatively trusts

    Unconditionally understood

Welcomes wounds

    Amazingly affirmed

       Crushed caterpillar

Ambushed attorney

       Buried barrister

Crushed caregiver

       Damaged deliverer

Empty esquire

       Fractured fighter

Grieving giant-killer

       Hopeless humanitarian

Insecure idealist

       Lost lawyer

Massacred messenger

       Needy negotiator

Orphaned orator

       Poisoned peacemaker

Ridiculed rebel

       Shattered shepherd

Traumatized truth-teller

       Unimaginably uplifted

Verbalizes value

       Wondrously weak

Absolutely accepted

At   tach   ment   dis   order

                        By kg

"into the wild"

                                        Ripped my heart out

'cause I don't wanna

              Need nobody

     For nothin'

'cause I was 9 months

           In the cocoon

     Of the womb

                                        Only to be torn away

                            From the only heartbeat

                                I'd ever known as home

'cause I was 11 months

         Being swung

Back   &   forth

     By

Mum   &   diane

                                      Only to be stolen away

                              From the only swing-set

                                  I'd ever known as safe

I became

    THE STRONG ONE

Speaking   seldom

    Listening   &   learning

Observing   &   disappearing

    Reading   &   remembering

Writing   &   hiding

I became

    THE SMART ONE

'cause if I could think

                             I'd never need to feel

I became

    THE ATHLETE

'cause if I could just

    Keep on runnin'

                           I'd never need

                 To
                     S
                      l
                       o
                        w

                              D
                               o
                                w
                                 n

I became

    THE HEALER

'cause if I could just

    Heal others' hurts

                    I'd never need

                To heal my own

But 1st year law

    Shattered my

Academic façade

                & forced me to feel

& running the marathon

    Shattered my

        Knees

                & forced me to crawl

& some peoples' pain

    Just couldn't be cured

                & forced me to face

                  My own fears

    I am terrified   of abandonment

& am unable to connect   with others

    For by keeping   my distance

```
I avoid                                         the pain
        Of                              separation
I became
        THE LONER
Never needing                           anyone
        Craving                         solitude
Yet yearning                            for connection
        For the kind of
Emotional nakedness
        That only seems possible
                                        With strangers
Yet fearing
        Being smothered
By this very same
        Connection

So truly yearning for
                A       shared          solitude
Where 2 souls
                Can     swim            together
In silence
                Hearing    in    each   other
                        The only heartbeat
                        They've ever known as home
```

   Transcending trauma

Wind-swept waves
   Treachery torments
Navigates neediness
   Stillness struggles
Chaos calms
   Shattered self-sufficiency
Traumatically terrified
   Stillness survives
Tentatively trusting
   Incarcerated idealist
Disillusioned donor
   Brutally broken
Orphaned openness
   Sacrificially selfless
Walking wounded
   Lost livelihood
Ruined reputation
   Imagines immortality
Transcends trauma
   Rebelliously redeemed
Spectacular sunset

        Vulnerable victor

Vulnerable servant
        Addictively ambitious

Damaged defender
        Openly orphaned

Compassionately conflicted
        Empathetically engaged

Painfully powerless
        Terrifyingly trusting

Hides heart
        Forgiveness frees

Surrender saves
        Unconditionally upheld

Prison break

Mystical prison

    Institutionalized emotions

Intellectually expressive

    Aggravates authorities

Buries brokenness

    Creatively chaotic

Distrusts discipline

    Embraces emptiness

Fears fragility

    Glimpses grace

Hides helplessness

    Loathes legalism

Militantly misunderstood

    Navigates neediness

Openly orphaned

    Passionately peaceful

Quietly questioning

    Relationally ruptured

Serenely struggling

    Tentatively trusting

Unconditionally upheld

        Divine desires

Selfish freedom

        Divine madness

Craves chaos

        Seeks stillness

Desires drown

        Navigates needs

Materialistic massacre

        Rational rapists

Soul survives

        Truth transcends

Unconditionally upheld

        Vulnerability vindicates

Welcomes wholeness

Welcoming weakness, part 2

Healthy doubt
      Ecstatically embraced
Craves control
      Love liberates
Fear fragments
      Hope heals
Strength stumbles
      Welcomes weakness
Condemnation cripples
      Mercy melts
Tragedy torments
      Humor heals
Transcendently trusting

                        Tsunami surfer

                Intimacy intimidates
                        Closeness confuses
Connection challenges
                Orphaned oneness
Independence invigorates
                Fragile father
Missing mother
                Loses love
Heart hungers
                Traumatically thirsty
Surfs tsunami
                Adores abuser
Welcomes wounds
                Denies distress
Riptides ravage
                Creditors crucify
Bankruptcy beckons
                Acknowledges abuse
Seeks safety
                Trusts tenaciously

       Embracing emptiness

Painfully present

       Abusive anchor

Victimized vulnerability

       Powerlessness paralyzed

Blindly betrayed

       Suicidally stubborn

Embraces emptiness

       Welcomes woundedness

Expressiveness energizes

       Stillness soothes

Forgiveness frees

       Peacefully present

Melodious mind

Abandonment aches
    Bawling baby
Careful child
    Damaged delinquent
Escapes emptiness
    Fears fragility
Glimpses grace
    Hides heart
Imagines innocence
    Juvenile joy-rider
Kennedy's killing
    Legalized lawlessness
Melodious mind
    Naively narcissistic
Orphaned openness
    Painfully present
Quietly questioning
    Resists regimentation
Seeks stillness
    Trusts tenaciously
Unconditionally upheld
    Vulnerability vindicates
Welcomes wholeness

        Divinely rebellious

Dying God

        Trust terrifies

Abandonment's anguish

        Desperately dependent

Powerlessness paralyzes

        Acknowledges anger

Survives sorrow

        Learns laughter

Communicates chaos

        Fears failure

Desperation dignifies

        Welcomes waywardness

Transcendently traumatized

        Divinely delivered

Rebelliously reborn

       Battling blindness2

Wounded wolf

       Betrayal blindsides

Hateful hunters

       Celebrate capture

Imprisoned idealist

       Damaged defender

Glimpses grace

       Escapes emptiness

Forgiveness frees

       Harbors hope

Battles blindness

       Communicates compassion

Destroys deafness

       Embraces enigmas

Finds friends

       Grasps grace

             Hobbles homeward

       Vocalizing vulnerability

Drowning depths

       Despair's deliverance

Vocalizes vulnerability

       Hears hunger

Sees slavery

       Poverty paralyzes

Shattered servant

       Hobbled healer

Utterly uncertain

       Shifting seas

Abusive anchor

       Bares bruises

Craves connection

       Desires deliverance

Escapes enslavement

       Flees facades

Embraces emptiness

       Destroys delusions

Calms chaos

       Breathes beauty

Absolutely accepted

"Orphaned heart"

Orphaned heart

    Plays alone

Laughs longingly

    Dances dramatically

Sings sorrowfully

    Demands distance

Escapes emptiness

    Runs restlessly

Hides horrors

    Survives stresses

Traumatically tortured

    Angrily anguished

Beautifully broken

    Chillingly challenged

Defiantly delivered

    Embraces emptiness

Finds fulfillment

    Glimpses grace

Opens heart

"Humor heals"

Intuitively nightmarish

    Imaginatively tragic

Enthusiastically visionary

    Futuristically focused

Spontaneous solicitor

    Openly orphaned

Abusively anchored

    Blindly battered

Chaotically crushed

    Deceptively destroyed

Enthusiastically emptied

    Finds friends

Glimpses grace

    Humor heals

"Energizing emptiness"

Comically catastrophic

    Melancholy masterpiece

Tragically transformative

    Angrily attacked

Brutally beaten

    Cruelly crucified

Divinely dependent

    Emptiness energizes

Fractures facades

    Graceful gambler

Heavenly hobo

    Inspiringly insignificant

Jams joyously

    Longing lacerates

Madness mobilizes

    Negates numbness

Orchestrates openness

      "Exquisite agony"

Beautifully brutalized

      Compassionately crucified

Divinely destroyed

      EMBRACED ENEMIES

Gloriously gory

      Hellishly honored

Mercifully massacred

      Necessary nightmare

Redemptively ruined

      Sacrificially slaughtered

Transcendently tortured

      Tragically transformed

            Beautifully broken

      Traumatically trusting

            Divinely delivered

                  Rebelliously resurrected

      Longing lacerates

Wrongfully judged

      Diabolically destroyed

Senselessly suffering

      Painfully prolonged

Treacherously traumatized

      Righteously ruined

Orphans openness

      Numbs neediness

Misses mercy

      Longing lacerates

Immeasurably injured

      Horrified heart

Genuinely guarded

      Fearfully fragmented

Escapes emptiness

      Detachment dignifies

Craves compassion

      Beautifully broken

Achingly acknowledged

"Perversely poetic"

Agonizing awareness

    Exquisitely empty

Divinely devastated

    Perversely poetic

Nobly naked

    Horrifically helpless

Loss liberates

    Unnervingly uncertain

Graciously grieving

    Compassionately crushed

Transformatively tormented

    Sublimely suffering

Welcomes wounding

    Transcends trauma

Creativity caresses

    Bathes brokenness

        Acknowledges anguish

            Breathes beauty

"Savage beauty"

   Annihilating mercy

      Embraces emptiness

Demonic blindness

   Imprisons imagination

      Chaotic kindness

   Illuminates injustice

Persecutor preys

   Persecuted prays

      Embraces enemies

   Defies demonizers

      Challenges complacency

         Brilliantly broken

           Achingly absolved

"Hobbled healer"

Shattered trust
    Destroys creativity
Accused advocate
    Hides heart
Struggling servant
    Imagines innocence
Damaged defender
    Divinely delivered
Hobbled healer
    Hopes heroically
Broken barrister
    Battles bravely
        Wounded warrior
    Screams silently
        Pleads poetically
            Aches artistically
                Melts mercifully

"playful god"

Allows anarchy

    Barbeques burgers

Catches throws

    Desires dialogue

        Encourages enigmas

    Forgives failures

Grieves gallantly

    Heals hurts

        Inspires imagination

    Jams joyously

Laughs lustily

    Makes macaroni

        Negates normalcy

    Ordains openness

Plays pool

    Questions quietly

        Rapturously rebellious

    Sings off-key

Treasures theorists

    Uplifts unconditionally

        Values visionaries

            Welcomes wounded

                Accepts absolutely

"servant shaman"

Articulates anguish

    Binds bruises

Compassionately contemplative

    Divinely dependent

Embraces emptiness

    Forgives frailty

        Glimpses grace

    Heals hopelessness

Illuminates injustice

    Jams joyously

Listens luxuriously

    Mourns majestically

Navigates neediness

    Openly orphaned

Painfully present

    Questions quietly

Risks rejection

    Shares sufferings

Trusts traumatically

    Understands ugliness

        Welcomes woundedness

        Whispers wholeness

"Elevating emptiness"

Suffering adventurer

    Serving explorer

Mentoring discoverer

    Spiritual gambler

Passive warrior

    Fragile fighter

Fears love

    Power poisons

Wisdom whispers

    Wounds weaken

Accusations ambush

    Falsehoods fragment

Battles blindness

    Craves community

Demands dignity

    Elevates emptiness

Faces fears

    Glimpses grace

Heals hurts

    Turns tables

        Suffering saves

"Rebellious revival"

Wounded warrior

    Bravely broken

Fiercely frozen

    Cradles carnage

Misses meaning

    Business brutalizes

Trust terrorizes

    Abandonment aches

Solitude soothes

    Peace pursues

Finds friends

    Rebelliously revives

Dances delightedly

    Jams joyously

        Art awakens

"Fragmented fighter"

Shell-shocked soldier

    Traumatized truth-teller

Understands ugliness

    Vanishing visionary

Weakened warrior

    Illuminates injustice

        Harbors hope

    Gambles gymnastically

Fights fragmentation

    Escapes emptiness

        Demands dignity

    Craves connection

Battles blindness

    Attacks apathy

Misses mercy

    Navigates nastiness

        Orchestrates openness

    Perseveres painfully

        Rebels radiantly

"Beloved brokenness"

Supreme sacrifice
    Solitary sufferer
        Craves community
    Beloved brokenness
Imprisonment isolates
    Release rejuvenates
Trials torment
    Truth transforms
Hopelessness hardens
    Sharing softens
Fear fragments
    Imagination integrates
Accusations annihilate
    Understanding uplifts
Senselessness sickens
    Peace pursues
        Sacrificially sustained

"Transformative torment"

  Acknowledges anguish

      Baptizes brokenness

          Chaos creates

  Dogma destroys

      Embraces edginess

          Faces fears

      Gentleness guides

  Harpooned heart

Insanity invigorates

      Lunacy liberates

          Madness motivates

  Negates normalcy

          Openness orchestrates

  Perseverance penetrates

          Rebellion radiates

  Surrender saves

          Trust transforms

  Unconditionally uplifted

          Vindicates voiceless

              Whispers wholeness

"Scandalous grace"

Irreplaceable idealist
      Brutally bloodied
Front-line fighter
      Scandalously sidelined
Enemies exult
      Friends falter
Mourns magnificently
      Grieves gallantly
Doubt damages
      Fear freezes
Cruelty crushes
      Sinks slowly
Welcomes waves
      Floats freely
            rebelliously
    Rises

"Breathtakingly yearning"

Abandoned visionary
    Shattered introvert
Intuitively wounded
    Traumatized feelings
Ravaged healer
    Perceives misery
        Breathtakingly yearning
    Questions cruelty
        Acknowledges absurdity
    Embraces impermanence
        Destroys delusions
            Redefines reality
                Vindicated visionary

"slander awakens"
(inspired by psalm 35)

robbed joy

    maliciously magnified

dishonorable witnesses

    evil rejoicing

good distressed

    humiliated soul

silent bereavement

    shameful slander

        awakens rescue

  silent ravages

devising deceit

    quiet peace

        favors afflicted

            delivers vindication

                needy rejoice

"Painfully perceptive"

Painfully confused

    Senselessly empty

Self-destructively stuck

    Robotically regressing

Burns bridges

    Undeniably unworthy

Fearfully fatalistic

    Valueless visionary

Hopeless healer

    Isolation imprisons

Seeks solace

    Dives deeper

        Perceives pricelessness

"Magnificently mangled"

Ceaseless torment

    Affliction's crucible

Brutalized bondage

    Shockingly slaughtered

Unbelievable upheaval

    Accusatory agony

Sustained strife

    Demonic drudgery

Magnificently mangled

    Wearily wounded

Frustratingly frozen

    Desires deliverance

Craves compassion

    Glimpses gold

        Finally feels

            Hopefully heals

"Embracing embers"

Fateful futility
    Hopeless hunger
Relentlessly reflective
    Divinely doubtful
Endlessly experimenting
    Spiritually struggling
Demonically despairing
    Embraces embers
        Envisions ecstasy
    Tenderly thriving
        Delightedly diving
    Breathtakingly beloved
        Frolics freely
            Swims sensuously
                Recaptures rapture

"Beloved vulnerability"

Fatalistically fearful

    Darkly despairing

Agonizingly abandoned

    Traumatically trusting

Fights fragmentation

    Craves connection

        Perceives possibilities

    Embraces encouragement

        Hopes heroically

Unconditionally upheld

    Faces fragility

        Victoriously vulnerable

"Shockingly unbroken"

False certainties
    True uncertainties

Easily supported
    Riskily surrendered

Devastatingly weakened
    Shockingly unbroken

Attacks traumatize
    Response dignifies

Enemy demonizes
    Friends fortify

Wastefully distracted
    Gratefully reawakened

Self-pity suffocates
    Openness reactivates
        Imagination integrates
            Courageously celebrates

"Paradoxically peaceful"

Externally assaulted
    Internally restored

Noisily weakened
    Silently strengthened

Enemies celebrate
    Friends encourage

Clearly deprived
    Subtly sustained

Painfully paralyzed
    Paradoxically peaceful
        Radically resilient
            Shockingly shatterproof

"Wonderfully weak"

Painfully powerless
    Crushingly compassionate
Openly obscure
    Perilously poor
Fearfully fragile
    Destructively doubtful
Visibly vulnerable
    Falsehoods fracture
Enemies exult
    Counterfeit consolations
Numb neediness
    Wonderfully weak
        Humbly hopeful
    Divinely defended
        Prayerfully protected
    Graciously guided
        Compassionately caressed
            Achingly accepted

"Demanding deepening"

Worthless brokenness
    Unlovable orphan
Useless advocate
    Intolerable injustice
Loses liberty
    Depressingly distant
Radically rejected
    Self-destructively self-rejecting
Cursed calling
    Absurdly accused
Blindly blamed
    Seeks survival
        Demands deepening
    Painfully purified
        Crisis challenges
    Craves communion
        Silently sheltered
            Blessed brokenness

"Unbelievably unvanquished"

Wilderness wanderer

    Desert dweller

Drowning disciple

    Stolen strength

Forgotten freedom

    Fatalistically fearful

Tragically tormented

    Hobbled healer

        Hopes heroically

    Unbelievably unvanquished

        Copes creatively

    Communicates chaos

        Vocalizes viciousness

    Bravely battles

        Insanely inspired

            Absurdly awakened

"Rebelliously revealing"

Demonic drudgery
    Painfully predictable
Sorrowfully stuck
    Cursed changelessness
Boring bondage
    Fearfully fatalistic
Paralyzing purposelessness
    Relentlessly raging
        Occasionally opening
    Momentarily mobilizing
        Tentatively trying
    Sporadically succeeding
        Passionately pleading
    Clumsily creating
        Rebelliously revealing
            Triumphantly transcending

"Hell/heaven"

Hell's gates
    Overwhelmingly oppressive
Tearing down
    Darkly despairing
Unraveling hopes
    Disturbing dreams
Weaving weariness
    Stealing strength
        Resistance re-energizes
    Fights fatigue
        Dreams daringly
    Hopes heroically
        Believes belligerently
    Restores rebelliously
        Overwhelmingly open
            Heaven's gates

"Liberating captives"

Condemnation's captive
    Preoccupation's prisoner
Bitterness buries
    Unforgivingly unresponsive
Anger ambushes
    Self-righteously resentful
Stubbornly scornful
    Hatefully hardened
        Sorrowfully softened
    Humbly hopeful
        Genuinely grateful
    Calmly confident
        Forgivingly flexible
    Acceptance animates
        Freely focused
            Large-hearted liberator

"Rebelliously rebuilding"

Demonic drought
    Viciously vilified
Relentlessly ruined
    Forcefully fictionalized
Dramatically demonized
    Surrenders strongholds
Dangerously denying
    Fatalistically fatigued
        Surprisingly strengthened
    Achingly acknowledging
        Relentlessly resisting
    Stubbornly steadfast
        Traumatically truth-telling
    Rebelliously rebuilding
        Compassionately cradling
            Divine downpour

"Suffering strengthens"

Angrily attacked
    Spiritually suffocated
Stolen self-worth
    Wounds weaken
Traumatically terrorized
    Doubts damage
Fears fragment
    Persecution pulverizes
        Suffering strengthens
    Imagination integrates
        Confidence calms
    Trust transcends
        Brokenness blesses
    Forgiveness frees
        Surrender saves
            Lovingly liberated

"Sorrow softens"

Anxiety's assault
    Paralyzes potential

Doubts drown
    Worries weaken

Fears fragment
    Confusion chokes

Shame sinks
    Hiddenness hardens
        Sorrow softens

Forgiveness frees
    Clarity calms

Inspiration integrates
    Simplicity strengthens

Confidence climbs
    Passionately persistent
        Peacefully present

"Façade fragments part 2"

Heartbreakingly hopeless

    Devastatingly despairing

Painfully paralyzed

    Laceratingly lost

Relentlessly restless

    Achingly anxious

Traumatically tormented

    Absurdly accused

        Acknowledges absurdity

    Seeks solace

        Pursues peace

    Calmly confident

        Façade fragments

            Dances delightedly

                Hopes heroically

"Imagination Intercedes"

25 years?

    500 grand?

Arrogantly absurd

    Belligerently blind

Coldheartedly cruel

    Dogmatically deaf

Enemy exults

    Fearlessly fabricates

Gratuitously graceless

    Hatefully histrionic

Insanely incensed

    Imagination intercedes

        Humbly hopes

    Glimpses grace

        Fragility frees

    Embraces emptiness

        Diplomacy defuses

    Compassion caresses

        Brokenness blesses

            Achingly accepted

"Emptiness elevates"

Traumatically tragic
    Hopelessly handcuffed
Nightmarishly nasty
    Destructively despondent
Falsehoods facilitate
    Poverty paralyzes
Enemy exploits
    Emptiness elevates
        Patience penetrates
    Fractures falsehoods
        Illuminates injustice
    Defies demonization
        Neutralizes nastiness
            Hopes heroically
                Trusts transcendently

"Powerlessness preserves"

Traumatically driven
    Catastrophically cursed
Powerlessly paralyzed
    Obsessively orphaned
Fearfully fragile
    Cruelly crushed
Hatefully humiliated
    Arrogantly accused
        Humbly healed
    Prayerfully protected
        Forgivingly freed
    Adoptively accepted
        Powerlessness preserves
            Blessedly broken
                Transcendently open

"Resiliently rebuilding"

Angrily assaulted
    Viciously wounded
Devastatingly demonized
    Violently vilified
Coercively condemned
    Overwhelmingly ostracized
Hatefully hammered
    Spitefully shattered
        Prayerfully persevering
    Resiliently rebuilding
        Craving community
    Supportively sustained
        Peacefully protesting
    Calmly correcting
        Hopefully healing
            Forgivingly embraced

"Rebellious refusal"

Coercive bondage

    Abusive enslavement

Rigid ruination

    Demonic deafness

Belittling blindness

    Murderous misdirection

Flagrant fabrication

    Destructive depression

        Rebellious refusal

    Truthful turnabout

        Resilient redirection

    Uplifting understanding

        Whispering wisdom

    Flexibly affirming

        Creatively encountering

            Lovingly liberating

"Miraculously meaningful"

Destructive disciplinarian
    Structured slaughter
Orderly obliteration
    Responsible ruination
Meaningless massacre
    Intimidating intransigence
Traumatically threatening
    Coercively condemning
        Rebelliously resisting
    Radiantly reassuring
        Creatively challenging
    Miraculously meaningful
        Responsibly reclaiming
    Disorderly deliverance
        Chaotically confronting
            Creatively liberating

"Tsunami surfer2"

Tsunami swallows

    Injustice infuriates

Lies lacerate

    Defensiveness destroys

Suspicion strangles

    Blindness brutalizes

Deafness decimates

    Fear freezes

        Love loosens

    Communication clarifies

        Verbalizes visions

    Intimacy intimidates

        Vulnerability vindicates

    Truth triumphs

        Justice celebrates

            Surfs tsunami

"Institutional Injustice"

Destructively deceptive

    Intransigence intimidates

Formidably fear-mongering

    Endless emptiness

Pointless persistence

    Suspicion suffocates

Betrayal blindsides

    Institutions infuriate

        Acknowledges agony

    Begs bitterly

        Confesses cowardice

    Desires deliverance

        Emptiness elevates

    Forgives enemies

        Forgives friends

            Releases rage

                Glimpses grace

"Surprising survival"

Terrifyingly tortured

    Overwhelmingly oppressed

Brutally betrayed

    Malevolently misunderstood

Deliberately demonized

    Futility fragments

Power pulverizes

    Self-righteousness slaughters

        Surprisingly survives

Weakness whispers

    Imagination integrates

Humility humanizes

    Benevolently broken

Gently guarded

    Expresses emptiness

        Craves communion

           Transcends trauma

"Embracing dawn"

Sunset strips
    Losing everything
Fearing catastrophe
    Fraudulently framed
Deceptively destroyed
    Silently slaughtered
Mercilessly massacred
    Abandonment's anguish
        Painfully perseveres
    Mercifully manages
        Vocalizes viciousness
    Destroys deceptions
        Rebelliously re-frames
    Vulnerability vindicates
        Climbs courageously
            Embraces dawn

"Achingly authentic"
(birthday poem 2011)

achingly anxious

    bracingly burdened

chaotically compassionate

    desperately dancing

ecstatically embracing

    frantically forgiving

generously grieving

    heartbreakingly hopeful

insanely idealistic

    jaggedly jarring

killingly kind

    longingly lingering

madly mindful

    needily numbing

openly orphaned

    painfully perceptive

quietly questioning

    reflectively robust

stubbornly single-minded

    tenaciously tender

urgently undaunted

    vainly villified

achingly authentic

    beautifully broken

His plan?

(inspired by a personalized license plate I saw yesterday)

"The mystical splendor of God will first burn us down, melt away all that does not belong to us, shear us of everything that we thought necessary for life, and destroy everything that is not pure gold." (morton kelsey, caring, page 6)

blindly burning

    mercilessly melting

savagely shearing

    deafly destroying

silently slaughtering

    apathetically abandoning

dogmatically drowning

    righteously ruining

        rebelliously resisting

    understandingly uplifting

        passionately preserving

verbalizes viciousness

    hears helplessness

soothes suffering

    compassionately cooling

        blissfully bathing

            angelically accepted

"Pursuing purpose"

Deafness devastates
    Blindness brutalizes
Abusively apathetic
    Carelessly crucified
Mindlessly massacred
    Senselessly slaughtered
Agonizingly abandoned
    Emptiness engulfs
        Escapes emptiness
Craves connection
    Pursues purpose
Miraculously mindful
        Compassionately crawling
Binds brokenhearted
    Envisions embrace
        Poetry penetrates
            Resiliently rebuilds

"Brutally betrayed"

Apathetically abandoned

    Brutally betrayed

Coercively crushed

    Deceptively destroyed

Erroneously erased

    Faithlessly forsaken

Gruesomely garroted

    Hatefully harpooned

Harbors hopelessness

    Grieves gallantly

Forgiveness freezes

    Embraces emptiness

        Desires deliverance

    Craves compassion

        Binds bruises

Awaits answers

"Judas' kiss"

god MONEY

    annihilates love

betrays trust

    crushes compassion

destroys dialogue

    erases empathy

fractures friendships

    generates guilt

        God LOVE

    Glimpses grace

        Falteringly forgives

    Empathy elevates

        Deepens dialogue

    Compassionately cradled

        Tentatively trusts

            Faces fears

                Hobbles homeward

"Tsunami Surfer3"

Fierce swimmer

    Heart's womb

        Warm soul

            Rhythmic mind

        Frustration swings

    Fights darkness

        Spinning angels

    Adoptive shell

Engages enemy

    Anger animates

Sorrow stimulates

    Rage rejuvenates

Loss liberates

    Fear fascinates

        Grasps grace

            Surfs tsunami

"Passionately persevering"

Brutally betrayed

    Callously crushed

deceptively destroyed

    fearfully fractured

greedily guillotined

    hatefully harpooned

indifference immobilizes

    laziness lacerates

        passionately persevering

    compassionately courageous

        lovingly listening

    provocatively powerless

        heroically hopeful

    truthfully transcending

        openly orphaned

            traumatically trusting

"Hungrily hopeful"

Destructiveness drowns

    Separation sinks

Hatred harpoons

    Fear freezes

Anger atrophies

    Depression distances

Ruinously rejected

    Brutally bastardized

        Amazingly adopted

    Compassionately cherished

        Closeness comforts

    Passionately peaceful

        Hungrily hopeful

    Lovingly liberated

        Connectedness climbs

            Creativity cascades

"Openness persists"

Arrogantly blind

    Cruelly deceptive

Empty façade

    Guillotines heart

Indifference jeopardizes

    Kills love

Numbs mercy

    Openness persists

        Questions ruiners

            Surfs tsunami

                Understanding vindicates

                    Wondrously yearning

"Family desserts"

Ecstatically painful
    Shattered trust
Sacrificially slaughtered
    Friends flee
Family desserts
    Darwin's desert
Enemies exult
    Craves connection
        Desires depth
    Explores emptiness
Fragility frightens
    Glimpses grace
Hides heart
    Imagines innocence
        Jams joyously

"LIVE"

Love

Indifference or

Violence

Embraces everyone eventually...

"redemptively ruined"

abusively apathetic
    blindly belligerent
coercively confrontational
    destructively dependent
fearfully frozen
    guiltily guillotining
heartlessly hiding
    imagines innocence
        jams joyously
    music medicates
        navigates nastiness
    openness orchestrates
        painfully perceptive
            quietly questioning
                redemptively ruined

"Darwin's Desert"
(title poem for 3rd part of poetic trilogy)

wilderness wanderer

    traumatically tragic

vulnerability vindicates

    understandably untrusting

sacrificially self-destructive

    romantically ruined

painfully paralyzed

    orphaned openness

navigates neediness

    mercy mobilizes

        loss liberates

    imagination inspires

        humbly hopeful

genuinely grieving

    faces fears

emptiness elevates

    desert dignifies

cactus cradle

    cradles coyote

        brokenness beautifies

            angelically abandoned

"navigating nonconformity"

resentment ruins

    hostility hardens

anger atrophies

    blindness brutalizes

cruelty crushes

    isolation imprisons

disastrously despairing

    viciously victimized

shell-shocked survivor

    navigates nonconformity

        transforms tragedy

    rewrites ruination

        dignifies despair

    confronts cruelty

        battles blindness

    addictively hopeful

        vocalizes voicelessness

            vulnerability vindicates

"salvaged swing-set"

shattered swing-set
    abandonment's anguish
brutalized boy
    crushed child
demonized disciple
    emptiness engulfs
forsaken fighter
    traumatized truth-teller
        tentatively trusts
  fragility frees
    embraces emptiness
  demands dignity
    cradles child
brokenness beautifies
    angelically accepted
        salvages swing-set
            surfs sunset

"piercing prejudices"

alienated adoptee
    blindly brutalized
fearfully frozen
    indifference isolates
loneliness lacerates
    prejudice pierces
solitude separates
    tragically traumatized
        unconditionally upheld
    vocalizes voicelessness
        welcomes wounded
    youthfully yearning
        tenderly transforming
    simplicity sustains
        pierces prejudices
            angelically adopted

"authenticity agitates"

injustice imprisons
    vulnerability victimizes
trauma terrorizes
    suffering subjugates
moralism massacres
    legalism lacerates
artificiality alienates
    powerlessness paralyzes
        authenticity agitates
    brokenness beautifies
        control crumbles
    destitution dignifies
        emptiness elevates
    facade fragments
        glimpses grace
            vulnerability vindicates
                love liberates

"imagination infiltrates"

(in solidarity with the "american autumn")

rationality ravages

    absolutism alienates

bureaucracy brutalizes

    conformity crushes

dogma decimates

    efficiency eviscerates

finality forsakes

    greed gentrifies

intellect imprisons

    imagination infiltrates

        generosity gives

    faithfulness forgives

        emptiness elevates

    dialogue discovers

        creativity caresses

            brokenness beautifies

                anarchy accepts

            raves rejuvenate

                spirituality sustains

   "wounded warrior"

lost lawyer
   masks melancholy
navigates neediness
   openly orphaned
painfully perceptive
   quietly questioning
ruined reputation
   stricken shepherd
     suffering strengthens
trauma toughens
   understands ugliness
vulnerability vindicates
   wounded warrior
yearns youthfully
   redemptively ruined
     liberated lawyer

"struggling servant"

thunderstorm swimmer

    tsunami surfer

wilderness wanderer

    achingly abandoned

desperately driven

    frantically fearful

        forgiving father

    divinely delivered

        achingly accepted

    obediently open

        courageously compassionate

            struggling servant

"Gracefully genuine"

(aka: 2 years in hell)

arrested advocate

    betrayed barrister

condemned criminal

    destroyed defender

evil exploiter

    forsaken friend

greedily guillotined

    hated helper

injustice imprisons

    imaginatively insulated

        humorously healing

    gracefully genuine

        forgives fragility

    embraces enemies

        defends dignity

    courageously compassionate

        bravely battles

    answers accusers

        appreciates angels

            transcends trauma

"acknowledging anger"

fearing failure

    masks medicate

misunderstandings magnify

    impatience injures

risks rejection

    acknowledges anger

        redirects rage

    imagines innocence

        mediates misunderstandings

    mercifully meditative

        forgiveness frees

"enigmatically expressive"

darkly healing

    absurdly hopeful

traumatically trusting

    love lacerates

suffering simplifies

    ruination redeems

wounds warn

    enigmatically expressive

money murders

    music mediates

conformity crushes

    creativity caresses

transformatively truthful

    mindfully mystical

        courageously child-like

"humanizing demons"

(a halloween poem)

power paralyzes

    fear freezes

greed gentrifies

    money murders

abusiveness angers

    blindness brutalizes

coldness crucifies

    pride punishes

damage demonizes

healing humanizes

humility honors

compassion comforts

brokenness beautifies

anger affirms

relationships resurrect

sacrifice strengthens

trust thaws

forgiveness frees

love liberates

"dreaming deliverance"

mistrust massacres

    shame shackles

doubt debilitates

    guilt guillotines

inferiority inhibits

    masks manipulate

isolation insulates

    self-absorption stagnates

despair destroys

    dreams deliver

        trust transforms

    autonomy asserts

        initiative inspires

    industry creates

        identity sustains

    intimacy illuminates

        creativity procreates

            integrity elevates

                hope heals

"radically accepted"

isolation conceals
    money murders
legalism lacerates
    moralism massacres
apathy annihilates
    superiority strangles
disdain destroys
    rejection radicalizes
        acceptance affirms
    compassion creates
        humility honors
    empathy embraces
        forgiveness frees
    spirituality sustains
        love liberates
            intimacy connects

"hobbled healer2"

abandonment aches
    betrayal blindsides
craves control
    dangerously dependent
eggshell ego
    fragility frightens
hides hurts
    isolation infantilizes
        intimacy integrates
    hobbled healer
        faces fragility
    embraces emptiness
        divinely dependent
    calmly chaotic
        blurs boundaries
            achingly authentic
                angelically accepted

"facades fragment"

agonizingly abused
    brutally betrayed
chaos consumes
    depressively disconnected
emptiness engulfs
    fears feelings
intimacy intimidates
    loneliness lingers
numbs neediness
    welcomes walls
        facades fragment
    navigates neediness
        solitude strengthens
    intimacy interconnects
        frees feelings
    embraces emptiness
        dances disconnectedly
    chaotically connected
        beautifully broken
            authentically adorable

"illuminated inmate"

lost liberty

    control collapsed

broke barrister

    integrated inmates

authorities annihilate

    demonized defender

eviscerated ego

    fragile fighter

        faces fragility

    embraces emptiness

        defends defenseless

    angers authorities

        illuminates injustice

    blurs boundaries

        calms chaos

            loss liberates

"challenging complicity"

embattled ego
    defensive defender
cowardice corrodes
    broken barrister
avoids anger
    accepts abuse
fears fragility
    hides hurts
hates hiddenness
    faces fragility
        acknowledges abuse
    affirms anger
        battles bravely
    challenges complicity
        demands dignity
            embraces empathy

"chaotic, broken, abandoned heart"

"This is a short story of a chaotic heart…

    a broken heart…

        an abandoned heart….

            it can be any heart, but it happens to be my heart…

…this heart was abandoned at birth
    fostered by grace for 11 months…
        and then adopted by a head & heart…
            which created chaos for this careful heart…
    so this heart became a strong heart, a heart which would never allow itself to be broken again
        …or so it thought

…and so in order to never be broken again, this heart disappeared inside its head…

until one day the head fell apart,
    and only the heart which had adopted it
        could resurrect the heart which lay buried beneath the rubble
            …and so this careful heart was reborn for a season…
        until one day the heart which had adopted it was buried beneath the load of a logging truck…
            and the heart then buried itself still deeper underground, vowing never to be broken again

        …until one day the heart which had been forced to abandon it at birth found its way back to it
        …and the chaotic, broken, and abandoned heart found new life in the embrace of its abandoned, broken, chaotic mother's heart…"

"empathy emboldens"

felonious friend

    abusive anchor

blindly brutalized

    complacency corrodes

damagingly dependent

    enviously embittered

greedily guillotined

    hatefully harpooned

control collapses

    surrender saves

        love listens

    poverty pierces

        empathy emboldens

    divinely dependent

        compassionately courageous

    beautifully broken

        angrily authentic

            forgiveness frees

"chaotically connected"

isolation imprisons

    hides heart

grieves guardedly

    fears fragility

embattled ego

    denies dependence

craves connection

    bulletproof bravado

abandonment aches

    acknowledges agony

        breaks beautifully

    chaotically connected

        dependence dignifies

    embraces empathy

        fragility frees

    grieves gorgeously

        hates hiddenness

            interdependence invigorates

"hidden heart"

achingly adrift
    abuse angers
lost lawyer
    hides heart
embattled ego
    fragile father
hurts head
    horrifies heart
sorrow swims
    birthmother blesses
        surrender saves

"hope hungers"

addictively abandoned
    buries brokenness
craves control
    desires deliverance
emptiness engulfs
    fears fragility
greed guillotines
    hides heart
lust lacerates
    love liberates
        hope hungers
    grace glides
        faces fragility
    embraces emptiness
        desires delight
    courageously compassionate
        beautifully broken
            achingly accepted

"fearless child"

swingset sanctuary

    rising falling

        totally trusting

    risking rewarding

        hoping dreaming

    battling bullying

        writing rapturously

    throwing catching

        playing ecstatically

    diving deeply

crashing burning

    breathing calmingly

        sleeping serenely

            dreaming delightedly

www.ingramcontent.com/pod-product-compliance
Lightning Source LLC
Chambersburg PA
CBHW032057150426
43194CB00006B/564